Contents

What is a swarm?

Swarms are large groups of similar animals such as insects, birds and fish, all moving in the same direction. Some swarms contain just a few hundred animals, while off the coast of California, billions of shrimp-like **krill** gather together, turning the sea red.

You can see swarms in the air, on the ground and in the sea. Swarms can appear almost anywhere: from locusts in the desert all the way to mosquitoes in the **Arctic**.

Swarm of locusts

A swarm of bats leaves a cave in Texas.

Swarms can appear to move like one big animal, like the swarms created by millions of bats living together in a cave. A stream of bats forms huge rings that twist and turn, perhaps to confuse **birds of prey**.

Did You Know?

In 1869, giant swarms of ladybirds invaded England. The bugs lay in such great heaps on the streets of Ramsgate that a new job was created to remove them: 'Ladybird shoveller'.

Ladybirds swarm together in search of food.

Why do animals swarm?

Animals swarm for many reasons. Fish swim together for protection, as individuals are less likely to be eaten by **predators** when they are in a large group. Ants, termites and bees form a swarm when the **colony** they are living in gets too crowded.

About once every ten years, caterpillars called armyworms swarm across the United States to find food, stripping the leaves from trees, and covering roads and houses.

Which swarms travel the furthest?

Every year, more than 300 million monarch butterflies **migrate** from Canada to Mexico in a massive swarm. Some have even crossed the Pacific Ocean!

Monarch butterflies

Did You Know?

Swarming can make it easier to find a **mate** in the jungle. In Thailand, thousands of male fireflies gather in **mangrove** swamps, creating a glowing cloud above the water.

Did You Know?

In Canada, garter snakes swarm together in underground dens. For eight months they stay rolled up in balls to keep warm. In spring, they emerge together, like a great wriggling river.

Red-banded garter snakes make dens in **limestone pits**.

Why are swarms scary?

Have you ever walked through a cloud of flies? Imagine meeting a swarm of locusts so thick that it blocks out the sun!

Groups of stinging animals such as bees can be dangerous, but most swarms are trying to find food or a mate rather than hurt you.

Did You Know?

Perhaps the scariest swarms of all are groups of red-bellied piranhas that hunt together. These fish have a mouth stuffed with razor-sharp teeth. Luckily, attacks on humans are rare.

Red-bellied piranhas live in the Amazon River basin.

Swarm of locusts in South Africa

If you walk or cycle into a swarm of flies they can easily get into your mouth or up your nose. Now imagine millions of creepy-crawlies scuttling across the ground in a giant swarm!

What's the deadliest swarm?

The Australian box jellyfish is perhaps the deadliest animal that lives in swarms.

The sting of a box jellyfish is so poisonous it can kill a person in just 3 minutes. If you attack it, the jellyfish gives out a warning signal. This sends other jellyfish in the swarm into a breeding frenzy, creating millions more!

Jellyfish warning sign

9

What are the biggest swarms?

In 1954, a swarm of 5 billion desert locusts flew over Kenya. Another swarm was over 3,000 km long! Locusts only gather when rain creates fresh food in the desert. The longer it rains, the larger the swarm becomes. The locusts soon eat everything nearby and are forced to go on the move.

Plague of locusts in ancient Egypt

Did You Know?

In 1875, a swarm of over three trillion locusts flew down from the Rocky Mountains and gobbled up 45 tonnes of crops each day on the Great Plains.

Which cannibals swarm?

Millions of Mormon crickets crawl across western North America in **columns** up to 8 km long, in search of protein and salt. The insects have to keep marching fast. If they don't, hungry crickets behind will eat them.

Female Mormon cricket

X-Ray Vision

Hold this page up to the light and see what's swarming under the ground.

See what's inside

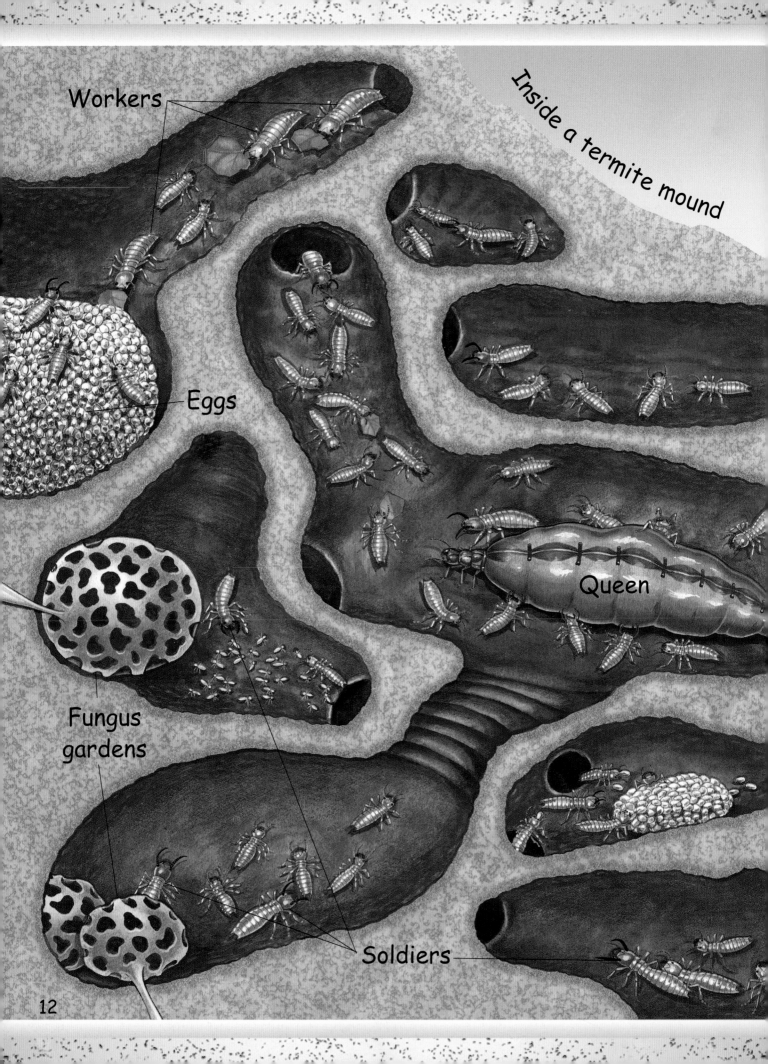

Workers

Eggs

Fungus gardens

Soldiers

Queen

Inside a termite mound

12

What swarms along highways?

Termites swarm to start new colonies. They can build huge mounds with long corridors. These corridors are connected by small openings that can be easily defended by soldier termites if the colony is attacked.

In the rainforests of South America, army ants swarm over the forest floor, eating everything in their path. The colony sends out 150,000 blind ants in a column up to 10 metres wide, which follow three-lane 'highways' laid down by **scouts**. They return in the middle lane, using their **antennae** to avoid bumping into other ants.

Army ants can kill spiders, scorpions, frogs and lizards.

Killer bees

Are bees dangerous?

Bee stings may be painful, but for most people they're not dangerous. If someone does die from a bee sting, it is usually because they are allergic to the sting. One man was stung 2,000 times and survived. To be safe, keep away from all bee swarms and hives.

What are killer bees?

Bees swarm when their colony gets too crowded. The **queen** leaves the nest with a swarm of **workers**. They cluster together while a few scouts find a good place for a new nest, such as a hollow tree. If you leave them alone, these swarms won't attack you.

So-called killer bees are honeybees which were brought from Africa to America by humans. They will chase you for nearly a kilometre if you get too close to their hive!

Did You Know?

Honeybees are very useful animals. They help **pollinate** flowers and provide us with honey and wax.

Yellowjacket wasp

A swarm of bees the size of a tennis ball contains around 3,000 bees, while a swarm the size of a basketball contains over 50,000.

Only honeybees swarm – wasps and bumblebees do not, though yellowjacket wasps will attack to protect their nest.

Swarming bees

What is the loudest swarm?

The mating call of the cicada is so noisy that it can drown out lawnmowers and telephones. If you had been in Indiana, USA in May 2004, you might have seen billions of cicada **nymphs** climb out of the soil and march up the nearest tree or pole.

These bugs spend 13 or 17 years underground before burrowing to the surface. They turn into adults, mate and lay eggs – all in just 10 days.

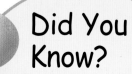

Did You Know?

Predators such as chipmunks and birds feed on cicadas until they can eat no more. Birds may become too full to fly!

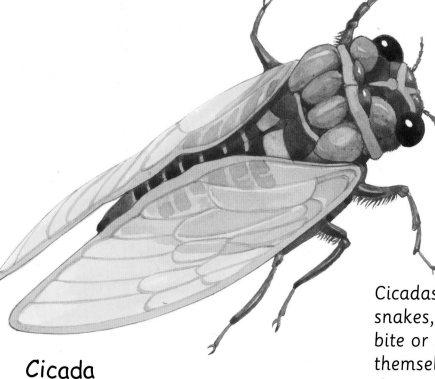

Cicada

Cicadas provide a feast for birds, snakes, moles and wasps. They don't bite or sting, but they defend themselves with sheer numbers. More than 1,000,000,000,000 (a trillion) can appear in just a few nights.

Like many cockroaches, the Madagascar hissing cockroach swarms, but it also makes a great pet! It lives up to its name by forcing air through holes in its body to produce a hissing sound when it is scared or when it is fighting.

Madagascar hissing cockroaches

Male frogs croak in a chorus to attract females. The tiny painted reed frog has the loudest frog call for its size. Males can be heard almost 2 km away from their pond.

Did You Know?

In the days before the earthquake that devasted Sichuan, China, in 2008, swarms of frogs were seen on the streets.

Croaking frogs

Why do birds flock together?

Birds flock together for food or safety. Starlings, blackbirds and pigeons all form huge **flocks** that wheel about in the sky or look for food on the ground. Gulls gather in big numbers on **mudflats** to feed.

Other birds nest together in enormous numbers for safety. Having many eyes together makes sure that some birds will spot predators while others are feeding, snoozing or just looking the other way.

Flock of starlings

Did You Know?

Flocks of birds such as ravens will attack and kill young lambs by pecking them to death, but it's very rare for flocks to attack people.

Flocks of snow geese

Some birds flock together to go on long migrations. Snow geese fly in flocks of 100 to 1,000 made up of many family groups.

They can fly for up to 70 hours, travelling 2,700 km from the Arctic to the Gulf of Mexico. They fly in a 'V' shape. This saves energy because the birds in the back can coast in the **slipstream** made by the birds in front of them.

Colony of northern gannets

Big colonies provide protection for seabirds, which are clumsy on land.

Bass Rock, off the east coast of Scotland, is home to 150,000 gannets. From a distance the island looks white because there are so many birds nesting on it.

What animals swarm in a school?

Fish can swim together in large groups known as **schools**, usually with other fish of a similar size and **species**. Most swim together for protection. A large school twisting and turning can look like a bigger animal, and this confuses predators.

Goldfish can find food more quickly in a big school. They alert others when they have found food by going into a 'head down' position. Swimming together may also help fish to save energy, by swimming in the slipstream of fish in front of them.

X-Ray Vision

Hold the next page up to the light and see why this school of fish is in danger.

See what happens

Did You Know?

A school is a tight group of fish moving as one. A **shoal** is a loose group of fish swimming together socially, rather than in order to protect against predators.

Pacific salmon live most of their lives in the ocean, but as adults they return to the stream where they hatched in order to lay their eggs.

Some migrate over 3,200 km then swim upstream, fighting **rapids** and leaping over waterfalls. They gather in huge numbers, **spawn**, and then die.

Spawning salmon

Sardines

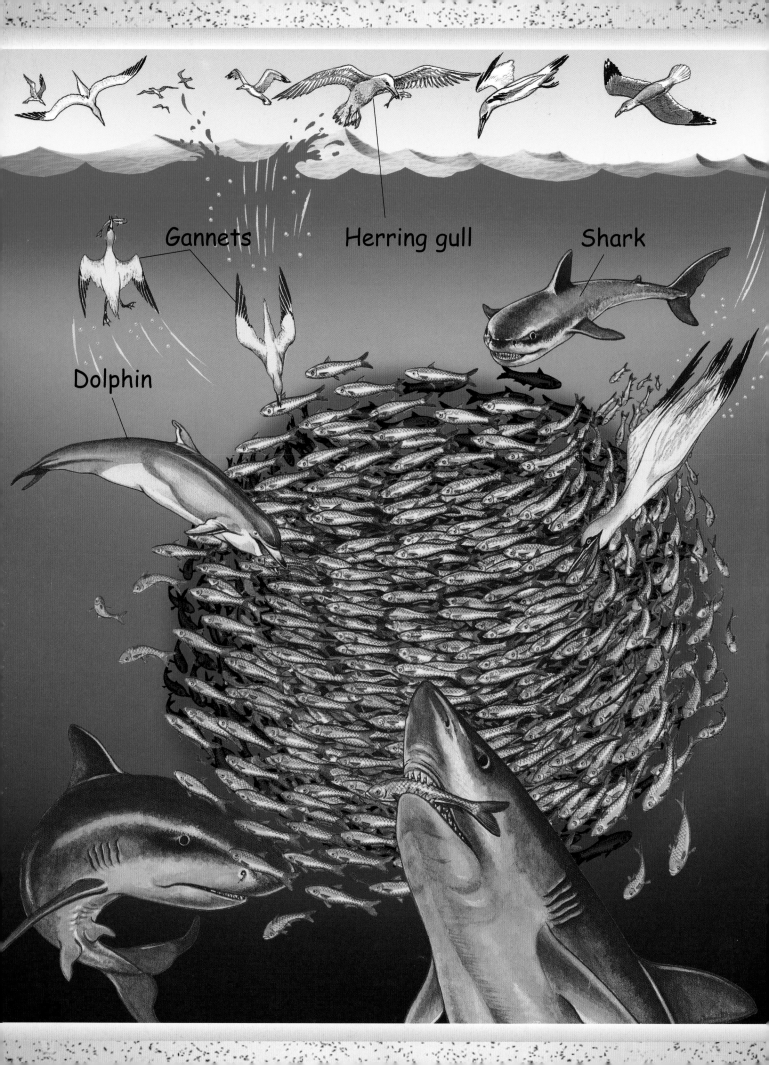

Gannets

Herring gull

Shark

Dolphin

What is a bait ball?

During an attack, some shoals of fish pack tightly together to form a school. Some schools do sudden U-turns or 'explode' as the fish swim in all directions.

A **bait ball** occurs when sharks and dolphins herd a shoal of sardines towards the surface and force them into a tight ball. Birds can spot the trapped sardines from the air. Sharks, dolphins and gannets all go into a **feeding frenzy**, gobbling up the sardines.

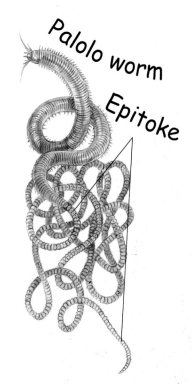

Palolo worm

Epitoke

Fish forming a defensive ball

What worm swarms?

The palolo worm digs into the coral of the Caribbean Sea, then waits until the one night in the year when conditions are just right.

Then the worm's rear end, called the epitoke, breaks off and becomes a separate animal! This swims to the surface and breeds in swarms.

Do lemmings really try to kill themselves?

Not really, no. Lemmings are small **rodents**, usually found in the Arctic. They have long, soft fur and very short tails. Lemmings spend most of their time on their own, meeting other lemmings only to breed.

However, every four years the Norway lemmings breed so fast that they are forced to migrate in enormous numbers. If a large group gets stuck in a small valley, they panic and flee in all directions. Some even swim across water.

Norway lemmings

Some people think that groups of lemmings purposely jump off cliffs. But lemmings don't try to kill themselves. What actually happens is that some are forced off cliffs when there are too many of them there.

Others drown when they are pushed into the sea as more and more lemmings arrive at the shore.

Other rodents live together in large numbers. According to the legend of the Pied Piper, the town of Hamelin in Germany had a plague of rats in 1284. Today many towns and cities have a similar problem.

In Mizoram, India, the government pays local people to kill the hordes of rats that thrive on bamboo crops that grow in the area. In Paris there are four rats to every human.

Did You Know?

In the summer of 2007, north-western Spain was crawling with 7.5 million voles. These furry rodents munched their way through wheat and potato crops.

In some Indian temples, the swarms of rats are sacred.

Do big animals swarm?

It's not just small animals that swarm – some grazing animals live and travel together in big numbers. In North America more than 120,000 caribou travel over 5,000 km each year in a giant herd.

They do this to get as far away from wolves as they can before giving birth to their calves.

Every year, 200,000 zebras and 400,000 Thomson's gazelles join 1.5 million wildebeest on a journey across the African plains. They travel in search of food and water, crossing baking plains and crocodile-infested rivers.

By keeping on the move, they stay one step ahead of predators such as lions and leopards.

A caribou herd crossing a river

Common dolphins

Do sharks swarm?

Yes! Several hundred adult lemon sharks swarm off the coast of Jupiter, Florida each year to find mates. Schools of up to 500 hammerhead sharks gather in the Gulf of California.

Hundreds of dolphins have also been known to gather in a school to feed together.

Did You Know?

Up to 500 white beluga whales can travel in groups called pods. Sometimes thousands join together in river mouths during the breeding season.

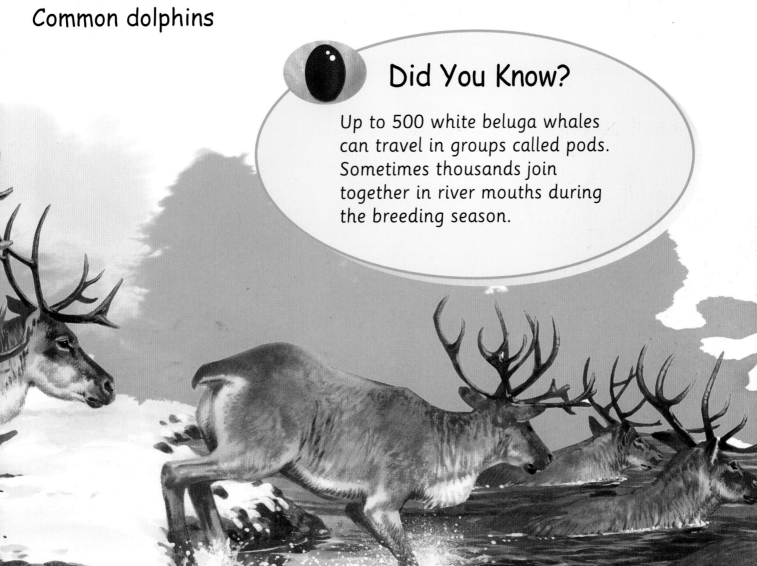

Can humans cause swarms?

Humans accidentally introduced yellow crazy ants to Christmas Island around 80 years ago. Soon the ants started to swarm.

Now super-colonies of the ant threaten the 100 million red crabs that leave the island's forest and crawl to the sea to breed every year.

In 1859, 24 rabbits were brought to Australia by a farmer. Within just a few years, millions of rabbits had spread across southern Australia, partly because there were no predators. Since then, by eating plants and destroying habitats, the rabbits have wiped out local species and put others in danger.

Red crabs crossing a road on Christmas Island, Australia.

Jellyfish in the sea off the coast of Norway

Yellow crazy ants get their name from their jerky, erratic movements. They live in nests of over 35,000 workers, attacking and killing spiders, **molluscs** and crabs by spraying acid from their bodies.

Yellow crazy ants

Can pollution create swarms?

The polluted waters near big coastal cities such as Tokyo, Sydney and Miami are attracting trillions of jellyfish. With no natural predators, swarms of them are hunting in packs and wiping out large shoals of fish.

Did You Know?

Global warming is also creating more insect swarms. In January 2007 a dry, warm winter led to a locust invasion in the Yucatán peninsula in Mexico.

Swarm facts

A locust swarm can quickly eat farmers out of house and home. In 1957, a single locust swarm destroyed nearly 170,000 tonnes of grain – enough to feed a million people for a year.

Flying swarms are often at the mercy of the winds. Over 100 years ago, a huge locust swarm in South Africa was blown out to sea. After tides swept the dead insects to shore, they formed a wall 1.2 metres deep which stretched for 80 km along the coast.

Columns of army ants can travel at speeds of up to 20 metres per hour and may contain 20 million ants.

Swarms of yellow crazy ants have killed over 20 million red crabs on Christmas Island in recent years.

Fire ants are red or yellow ants with a sting that burns like fire. They travel in swarms and can invade kitchens. They will also attack the young of ground-nesting birds, and even newborn kittens.

Cicadas come out of the ground in **broods**. Some broods appear every 17 years, others every 13 years. No one knows how they count the years. The biggest group, known as Brood X, will next appear in 2021.

In 2004, scientists glued tiny transmitters onto the backs of Mormon crickets to track their movements. They found that crickets who strayed from the main swarm were much more likely to be eaten by birds and other predators.

The weight of all the termites in Africa is greater than the combined weight of all the zebras, wildebeest, elephants and other grazing animals. That's a lot of termites!

In November 2007 a 15-km wide, 13-metre deep swarm of mauve stinger jellyfish attacked Northern Ireland's only salmon farm. The surrounding sea turned red with all the jellyfish.

Red-bellied piranhas hunt in groups of up to 100 fish. Like sharks, they are highly attracted to the scent of blood. The group spreads out to look for **prey**. When it is found, the scout signals the others, probably using sound, as piranhas have great hearing. Each fish rushes in to take a bite, then swims away to make way for the others.

Glossary

antennae Feelers on each side of an insect's head.

Arctic The icy region around the Earth's North Pole.

bait ball A group of fish forced to the water's surface by sharks or dolphins.

birds of prey Birds that are especially good predators.

brood A group of young, all born at the same time.

colony A group of animals living together. When several colonies of the same animal work together, they form a super-colony.

column A line of animals following one after the other.

feeding frenzy A situation where animals eat as much and as fast as they can.

flock A group of birds flying or feeding together.

global warming The gradual increase of the Earth's temperature.

krill Small, shrimp-like crustaceans that swim in huge swarms in Antarctic waters.

limestone pit A quarry or canyon made of limestone.

mangrove A tree that grows in dense forests, on coastal mudflats and swamps throughout the tropics.

mate A partner of the same species that an animal can reproduce with.

migrate To take a long journey to another habitat in search of food, to escape predators, or to find better weather conditions.

mollusc An animal with a soft body and often a shell, such as snails, slugs, squid and octopuses.

mudflat A muddy coastal area that forms when mud is deposited by the tides.

nymph The young of insects that look like their parents.

plague A huge number of animals that devastates a habitat.

pollinate To transfer pollen from one plant to another.

predator An animal that kills and eats other animals.

prey An animal that is hunted by other animals.

queen The only female that can breed in a colony of ants, bees or termites.

rapid A part of a river where the water flows very fast.

rodent A mammal, such as a mouse or rat, which has large teeth in its upper and lower jaws for gnawing food.

school A tight group of fish from the same species which moves and acts as one.

scout An animal that checks the area ahead for food or predators.

shoal A loose group of fish from the same species.

slipstream An effect caused when an animal pushes air or water out of its way, making it easier for the animals behind to gain speed.

spawn To lay eggs in water.

species A group of animals or plants that look the same, live in the same way, and produce young that do the same.

swarm A large group of animals moving in the same direction.

worker An ant, bee or termite that cannot breed but finds food and cares for the queen and her young.

Index